This Journal is the property of:

Your Free Gift!

Stay organized each week with our Weekly Planner

Download today at:

www.asselingroup.com/journals

Weekly Planner

For the week of: _____

To Do List

Time	M	T	W	Th	F	Sa	Su
9am							
10am							
11am							
12pm							
1pm							
2pm							
3pm							
4pm							
5pm							
6pm							
7pm							
8pm							

Download our Weekly Planner and also receive other free planners to keep you organized all year long (such as grocery shopping lists, birthday lists, holiday planners, and more)!

Made in the USA
Monee, IL
16 June 2023

35966488R10095